Dreams of the Deluded

Anshuman Gupta

BookLeaf Publishing

Presentation by *BookLeaf Publishing*

Web: www.bookleafpub.com

E-mail: info@bookleafpub.com

ISBN : 9789357210706

First edition 2022

DEDICATION

To Sanya Jalota, who encouraged me in the first place to carve out a canvas from my mind

To my Mom and Dad, for being proud of what I wrote without caring about it's quality

ACKNOWLEDGEMENT

Writing has been a journey to me that sort of always made sense as a natural progression of my passions but was something I was yet to seriously undertake in, until a certain someone pushed me to begin writing down various things for various reasons. Therefore I'd like to acknowledge this person, Sanya Jalota, for making me start writing a book in the first place and being my support partner throughout all of it, giving her criticial analysis of it and her viewpoints, something that mattered greatly to me as she was an incredible artist herself, be it poems or paintings.

I'd also like to acknowledge my parents, my Mom and Dad for being supportive of all my random stuff, even if they were confused by it. Thank you for hyping me up whenever I wrote random blogs for college clubs, thank you for hyping me up when I wasted my nights writing random poems, thank you for being so willing to hype me up in front of every other person they possibly could, I love you both so much <3

PREFACE

I honestly never started writing poems to have them published into a book one day, that's just an added bonus if I'm being honest. What I wanted was some sort of escapism, I've been an avid dreamer for as long as I can remember and as cliche and sweet as it sounds, it honestly became suffocating after a while how trapped I always was in my own imaginations, thoughts and fantasies. Getting a chance to escape them by penning them in the form of a poem was something that was so relieving to me, and well something that I feel would be 'fun' to share with others, maybe or maybe not. This is bound to be a wild ride at the very least!

Ascended Reality

It's a privilege to be able to live, that much is true
I'm special just for being born into this world, who can argue
Yet I feel no gratitude inside my special body
Hating this world, may be too melodramatic but it has become a hobby

You can't prevent me from feeling extremely bitter
Especially as I relate my entire existence to discarded litter
What a waste of energy it is to breathe in this society
So don't blame me when I try to ascend this very own reality

Where everything feels magical as I'm stuck in my self-made fantasy
I can write my own story to create results that are so satisfactory
Every moment of this simulation feels real and so perfect
The people here are flawless and true, people with whom I can connect

Maybe that's why it hurts when I forget all of it
is fake
Having unreal expectations from people who
never matched them in the first place was
perhaps, a mistake
I feel like I'm a success in this fake world as I
do everything I dreamt of and more
Meanwhile in reality I'm just laying in my bed,
dreaming while my body feels sore

Feeling low and depressed for no other reason
but my delusional mind
Which has written everything so damn
thoroughly the actual reality now feels so
confined
Being out with friends where I'm supposed to be
happy, joyful and most of all I should be grateful
Yet here I am zoning out trying to ascend once
again to the world where I'm not hateful

Burdening myself with a lone wolf act as I push
people away for no apparent reason
Never feeling I can connect permanently as my
mind brings forth its grievance
With the world around me being as it is and not
how it should be in my authored story
The story where instead of being a bore I
manage to grasp at glory

Realisation slowly crawls on me that this story
isn't a perfect world realised but rather an
excuse
A simulation to hide in, one where I may be of
some use
For even when there exists a person I can finally
permanently connect with, find peace as I drop
my disguise
The over-dependence on a single source of
happiness can oftentimes lead to its demise

The truth is that this ascended reality isn't a
haven but rather a prison
Where my doubts, fears, and insecurities haven't
been quenched but rather they've arisen
It's time I face the truth and accept the cold hard
fact
For as much as I pretend and hide, this is a
concept that really isn't that abstract

As in the dreams of an idealised flawless future
that is better than my past
I'm sleeping on my present and letting my dark
emotions everlast....

Mask Of The Deluded

Popularized enough as an accessory wore by the heroes to keep their loved ones safe
Hardly ever was spotlight given to the losers hiding behind it, much to their irate
Truth be told it's much easier to wear the mask and bear it all with the fakest smile
Convince everyone you're much better than what you actually are, show them your guile

Not sure if I wore it because I was insecure about the way I looked
Certainly not a fan of the person in the mirror, a being wretched and crooked
But I do seem to not care anymore, for looks seem a concept too superficial
So why am I still a person wearing a mask, acting as if I am artificial?

Evidently enough there isn't depth when it comes to who I am as a person
It really shouldn't be this complicated, yet this is a matter that still worsens
For just being me, a simple human seems too much like a chore

Very much comfortable hiding still, even if I
become a bore

I really do connect with you however, enough to
reveal my secret identity so as to speak
Which is really that of an awkward bumbling
boy, voicing his share of opinions with a squeak
Unmasking myself is something I enjoy, believe
me I do not like being suffocated
Consistency has never been the key for me
however, so I do understand you being frustrated

Honestly an overflow of emotions easily takes
me over as I try to control my tears,
Crying my heart out till the eyes hurt, I am numb
as I succumb to all my fears
Trust me honey, you're probably better off
avoiding me
Because tear away the smiley face I like to adorn
and there still would be nothing you'd like your
partner to be

Melancholy seems like a crutch these days as I
can slowly feel myself losing my entire soul,
Am I wearing a mask or is it just a false pretense
I use to pretend I'm actually whole
Mirror mirror on the wall when I look into it I
wonder whether I'd feel any affection

Guess I'd never know because I'm absolutely
terrified of my reflection

When it boils down to it I think my biggest fear
when it comes to you is quite simple,
It's not you lifting my mask and finding me to
be a cripple
If that was the case I know you'd still give me
an embrace
Rather, I'm afraid that someday you'll remove
my mask but end up finding no face…

Knights of Justice

Setting out in the merry road they have an air of confidence
Clasped in their tight armor they ride on their horses to gather some evidence
Of wrongdoings in the countryside for they are the harbingers of justice
They are the ones to protect their country, they will be the ones to root out all menace

Sword made of steel they unclasp as they set on the bandits that prey
On the innocents of the realm as for a savior they pray
Come the knights in shining armor, quite literally
Slashing the villains in two with skills formidable but deadly

Cheered by the crowds as they return home triumphantly
Their faces beaming with pride as they collect their coin happily
But one of the saviors could be least bothered by the bounty
All he's really in it for is the glory

For being the son of a merchant he knew the woes of the poor
Even after his father gained the favor of the King, he can't forget what it feels to sleep on the floor
"Never again", was the solemn promise he swore
As train with the sword he did, with determination and vigour

It was in the training courtyard that he met his brother
The son of a noble from a wealthy order
Representing all his desires the son of the merchant could feel his eyes gleam
Striking down the snobby rich, now that was a dream!

Charge he did waving his wooden sword with no sense of direction
Easily dispatched by the son of the noble, with utter humiliation
Spitting on the ground he had landed, he was feeling the urge to quit
When the unexpected happened as he looked up to see the hand of the person he had tried to hit

Rising up like a phoenix he began to train

With the aid of a noble, as the son of the merchant gulped down his vain
Months turned into years as a prominent warrior he became
But more important than his skills was the companionship he obtained

Close as brothers they cared not for the societal norms
For they were too powerful together, stronger than any storm
They needed no mistresses or privilege
They were content with just being the saviors of the village
So when calamity struck the nation, the gods seemed cruel
Fell their kingdom to traitors and ghouls
Escaped to the woods on their horses as the castle burned behind them
But for the merchant's son, more horrifying was being separated from his brethren

Rode as warriors without banners they did in the land which had now become alien
The only one the son of the merchant could trust was his missing companion
Weeks passed by as his survival was laid to the test

Being as skilled he was, hunted he was by the traitors, those miserable pests

But survived he did, still not sleeping on any floors
The trust of the common folk he had, who offered their huts with an open door
So his crusade against injustice continued, albeit this time alone
Missing his brother for he was now an incomplete soul

So when the reunion happened, the gods seemed kind
As when protecting a village the son of the merchant lost his mind
For there was his brother, with his sword and armor still intact
As the son of the merchant got off his horse and ran to him to initiate contact

Incapable he was of feeling anything but love and happiness
So oblivious he still was when the sword stabbed his body, sprouting out blood in all it's nastiness
Confused was his mind as he gazed at his brother with concern and surprise

Whose eyes seemed dull as he steadily held the sword of his brother's demise

For a person who had the comfort of possessing everything finds it easier to rebel
Which was why the son of the noble was comfortable in loving the son of the merchant as an equal
When fell the kingdom fell his comfort
The son of the noble was weak all along when in face of an actual hazard

Desperate to get back all he was he turned his cloak
Threw away all that was close to him as his kingdom burned to smoke
Happy enough to collect the bounty on the one he called a brother
Striking him down without any hesitation in an act that can only be described as callous

They say when detached from the body, the head is able to see only for a short while after death
Yet the son of the noble claims otherwise after witnessing an act that left him out of breath
For when dumping the head of his brother for the bounty, he saw something he swore
He saw tears in his brother's eyes, as his face was dumped onto the floor.

Woes Of The Saviours

Is it worth it to be free?
What exactly is the importance of liberty
Was it meant to be achieved through so much blood
Cries the soldier on top of corpses as the war ends and he's covered in mud

It wasn't easy as the fairytales make it seem that much I assumed
But to not even have a happy ending feels too much of a doom
There isn't any magical hair that will revive me from the dead
Cries the solider covered in wounds and grasping for breath

Are ideals more important than love?
Standing up for what's right in an uniform adorning the peace symbol of a dove
Yet losing what was mine in the house I left behind
Never again kissing my wife, having a child, that is too much to decline

Cried the solider, leaving for the first time to fight in a war meant to achieve freedom, yet himself he felt so confined

"WE ARE FREE" shouted the leaders as the parades cheered their name
The land is theirs as they plot their next move in what they call politics but actually is more akin to a game
For who cares about the pieces used for one's entertainment
It's the soliders who will be the ones to ultimately lose their freedom after all, tortured by their minds and the lives they took for an entire generation

Morality Of The Hero

Can rise up in the sky with little exertion, leaving behind a crater
Has the power to destroy mountains with a single punch, causing the people of this world to view him with terror
Is he a god or a demon, the masses preach their sermons with fervour
Maybe he's just a guy trying to do the right thing, is preached in return by the atheists with vigour
Can we expect a man to hold such power without any repercussions, cry the rulers
Constructing weapons against him is inevitable, say the fearers

Saving the day comes naturally to him as he prevents disasters upon disasters
And when the work is done flies back to his abode, the place where he stashed her
'Her' can be called the most broken person in the world
Who's still in bewilderment as to why she's chosen by the man who if he wills, can be the world's overlord

She looks at him with pity in her eyes for she
believes she brings his life to ruin
As she loathes the world as well for treating the
man she loves with such disgust and suspicion
How much more should he do to prove to you
he's humanity's most moral character
Anger as well she feels towards the hero for not
just letting the world fall into disaster

He comes towards her but she recoils back in
fear
Fear as she, the most broken person in the world,
predicts herself to be his downfall as if she's a
seer
Love she truly does feel for the man who always
comes down for her to stay at her side
Yet forget never can she the treatment he gets
but always puts aside
For she can never forget the day he came to
comfort her with all his strength
So deep in her pain she was all she could do was
keep him away in circumstances that became
intense
So accustomed to his strength she stopped
giving a care to his wounds
Throwing knifes at his face for she knew it won't
leave a scar is to what she became attuned

"Why do you continue to be a hero" she shouts
at him everytime he returns
"Why continue to love me" she cries to him
everytime for her, he yearns
For half the word despises him for daring to be
greater
Meanwhile all he's worried about is when she
would become better

Today was different as when he flew back the
hero was ready to tell her the truth
Why he's willing to don a cape and save the
world rather than enjoy his youth
She was prepared to listen to his morality, the
one she wishes to have so she can be of use
Yet what he answered was something which was
meant to confuse
He didn't consider himself a hero is what he said
and that caused her to snap
"You use your powers to help people, so cut that
humble act"

But he just shook his head and spoke once more
"Never did I say I was a villain as well intent on
making the world sore
The truth is I'm just a person who is bitter
Bitter at being who I am, I dreamed of just being
better
Not because I care about the world or it's people

They can burn down for all I care, as a species they are truly evil
I became a hero because I wanted to feel I am whole
For in actuality, I am the most broken person in this entire world"

She just stared at him with a loss as to what to say
As he came closer to her, this time she didn't immediately push him away
"My acts of heroism are a way to hide the devil inside of me
Maybe being the way I am let's me know you're not broken despite what in the mirror you may see
All I know is you are the only one I actually love in this whole wide world
Maybe proving to you I can save you is also why I wear the cape, besides just wanting to feel whole
So let me be in your life as well, I promise you are the only thing in this world that isn't a bother
If we are both shards of broken glass, how can we ever hurt each other?"

Tears formed in her eyes as she let herself in his hug

He held her tightly, feeling optimistic for once as everything inside of him he had dug
For despite being broken both of them could easily be fixed
He believed that truly, as he brought her closer to his lips....

The Letter

Clinging to the edge of the cliff I hold so dearly
Instead of looking down climbing right back up is what I fear so greatly
They say love is a dangerous game and I can feel my chest collapsing
They say facing your emotions is scary, and I already feel like I'm crashing
Yet here I am with my pen out why do I insist on writing?

Demons fight harder than ever even at a time I thought evil spirits I can't see
This leads to the age old conundrum of " it's not you, it's me"
I'm the evil incarnate loving you and yet still combating hatred
Being with an inconsistent person like me, how can anyone be satiated?

Why am I so full of these insecurities that want to weigh me down
I can be given the keys to my kingdom and still not be satisfied with my crown
Tossing the gilded cap away and leaving this throne room

Going back into my cabin at the end of the day and still feeling freaking gloom
So stuck with a terrible mess of mind I end up gurging out all these words
Words I desperately try to weave together no matter how absurd

But things still seem alright when I look at you
Gazing into your eyes and those brilliant two shades of hue
Day after day, month after month this desire for you only grew
With a stroke of the paintbrush this most beautiful canvas you drew

Ever the dreamer, frequent the fantasies
Only to wake up and add a pinch of honesty
Because come on man, let's be real
A guy like you and dreams of that deal?
Look at the woman of that stature
Deserving her fair prince in a knight of shining armour, not you, you freak of nature
Chasing dreams is all I ever have been able to achieve
Being worthless and needy as I crave for every trace of self-pity

Trust me your horror at my words is not something I deserve

I'm a guy who craves so much I get jealous at every turn
Your touches take me up to the sky as if I flew
A single piece of your attention makes my heartbeat increase by two
Every second spent alone with you makes me feel anew

Maybe I'm just always meant to be a question mark with the dot
Maybe I'm just the stain on your shirt, maybe you want to clean that spot
Maybe instead of the smile giver, I give you the frowns
Maybe instead of making you happy, I end up letting you down
Maybe I make you tensed, maybe I'm someone you want to avoid
Maybe that's why consistently you'd rather jump into someone else's arms to fill the void
One's too many the crowd
Walk fast and lose me, I'm not worth the sound
I'm not the person you love the most and consider your future
I'm that same old guy whose only worth is just being a watcher

Walk away little one it's time you resume your howling

For no matter how much you love her she doesn't deserve this monster prawling
Yet stay I want to for a little while and finish what I've started
This rainbow I see up in the sky is still where my heart is

Shining bright is something you subconsciously manage even when it's raining raindrops blue
Now it's my time to let this out and let my ugliest side break free
Cause this was never meant to be a love letter to you
Rather, this is a letter of self-loathing to me....

Balance of Yin-Yang

Love and hate are two emotions always written
to be in conflict with each other
They can be called polar opposites, are referred
to as each other's nemesis
Yet one supports the existence of the other for if
we never learned how to hate, how can we grasp
love?
If there didn't exist species confined to the land,
how can they evolve into creatures that can fly
like the dove?
Without resentment how can gratefulness thrive?
Without shocks to the body, how can a person be
revived?

Hate might as well be the absence of love
In myths, borne out of love is usually the origin
of a curse
Bitter is the person who has been refused the
taste of sweetness
Therefore, they have only been showered with
the taste of sourness
The balance of Yin and Yang teaches us that
opposite ideals are equal, none superior over the
other

Therefore to maintain balance, in existence
every emotion must birth another
Without the worst feeling in the body that burns
us up, how can we even fathom an emotion so
pure it soothes the soul?
How can we appreciate sweetness without
knowing how it feels to be sour?

The terrible truth therefore is, every person you
ever loved
Exists due to every person you ever hated and
shoved
Maybe pure love for a person can only exist if a
small portion of hatred is reserved for them in
your heart
Or maybe it's all the rambling of mad men
fantasizing what it means to love and everything
else surrounding that art

Optimism In My Consience

Is it justified to feel optimism as an option?
I ask myself as I read about the horrors going on in the world in that newspaper section
In a world where the good and bad often becomes blurred
Where any people different from what's considered normal are often times the subject of riducle and slurs
Where people have a problem with who is loved by whom
Where it is expected that a love story can only be accepted with a bride and a groom

Why should I have faith in a species that has so often adopted hate as a weapon
Destroying the environment for their own pleasure and leaving the land barren
Treating their own offspring as a property instead of their own person
Abandoning them for choosing their own path and letting their life worsen

Why should I believe in the human race when the term itself is so selective
Not meeting the beauty standards leads to you being declared a defective

When having a different skin colour is a crime
When being able to love someone of the same gender is a long grind

Why should I be happy to be born a man when I myself didn't get a say in the state I was born into
In a world where I'd have my identity forced onto me regardless of the image in the mirror I view
Where you either adhere to society or be deemed a freak
Where if you have the same collective opinion, only then you are allowed to speak

All of it does indeed seem overwhelming, faith seems like a lost dream, optimism feels like a joke
Yet here I am, call me naive but I still believe the human race isn't broke
For I have optimism in people rebelling against the injustices that trouble us so
For I have faith in the belief that every person can eventually grow
For I am happy to be born into this world for the bonds I have and the people I adore
For I believe in the good admist the bad, even if the boundary seems obscure

Truly we have advanced so much, our greatest strength is possessing sentience
As sentience means we have the liberty to have a moral conscience

This world was formed on a kill or be killed concept
Prey and predator is the origin of life and the food cycle existence is what makes me accept
That the universe was created on a cruel context
Where fittest of the survival was the world's way of having the weak and different be cleansed
Therefore the birth of humans having a moral compass is important
For our mind allows us to perceive the horrors created in this universe by the omnipotent

Disasters and hardships are often times a human invention
But love, understanding, hope and acceptance is also a human creation I say, in contention
Therefore Optimism is indeed an option and faith is prudent to have
For humans are of many types and peace and happiness can everlast
For while the lines between the good and bad are often blurred
Humans still try to make sense of it and help let the good preserve

Confused Identity

Greed is my worst enemy
Superficialness proves to be an adversary
My goal that I ultimately want to strive towards
is in conflict with my current trajectory
My emotions and thirst loves to play it's tricks
on me, wanting me to pursue illusions of what I
think will make me happy

My biggest fear is ruining what I actually love
for reasons that will ultimately leave me
unhappy when they become true
Superficial reasons that will with time become
unsatisfactory to pursue
But I'm no prophet how am I to know what is to
come
I'm not an analyst how am I supposed to know
what I actually feel and will become

Truth to be told I'm scared by the story of Icarus
and how he fell from the sky
He flew too close to the sun and ultimately fell
down to his death with the biggest cry
Am I already flying or am I still on the ground?

Dare I risk flying too close to the sun or do I
dare never to leave the ground and be forever
bound?

I love to preach stuff I myself never do
The hypocrisy in my mind continue to grew
Am I too greedy with my wants and desires?
Or am I too submissive to my fears and ire?

Am I a philosopher or just a wannabe?
Perhaps nothing about me is deep and I'm a
nobody
Do I actually think deep into my desires and
interests?
Or am I just superficial like the rest and being
different is something I just manifest?

Truth to be told I'm just a confused person who
likes to write
I have no clue whatsoever what is and what isn't
supposed to be right
I'm too impulsive to always listen to my mind
Too emotional to leave anything of my past
behind
So even if I take a stand I don't know what will
be the end result
Will I commit to it or will I find being consistent
still as difficult?

Curse Of A Werewolf

Under the crescent moon
A lonely shadow emerged
Shimmering in the moonlight
It let out a howl
A howl of sadness
A howl of pain
A howl of longing
A howl which marked it's suffering

They say wolves are proud creatures
They say wolves are full of vain
Spreading misery around them
With their cursed bites causing change
Turning humans into werewolves, the most cursed beings
For they are neither human nor animal
Nothing but an amalgam of shame

Always referred in myths as evil creatures
Basking in the glory of the horror of their prey
Yet the truth couldn't be further
When it came to this lone wolf
Like humans, wolves are many
Many natures, many personalities
They feel love, they feel pain

By causing terror they have nothing to gain

As the sun came up on the horizon
As the night faded by
The wolf changed form
Turning from a lonely beast to a lonely woman
Shunned by her village
The poor girl moved on
It wasn't her choice, this destiny of hers
It wasn't her choice to have this pain inflicted on her

The Japanese say the moon spirit too is a girl
Driven from her home for her duty, she too is alone
Maybe this is why the werewolf and the moon are related, both of them are lonely spirits finding kinship in each other
The girl wanted this kinship

But not with the moon, for she couldn't embrace it nor kiss it with the sweet taste of love
But only stare longingly at it as she cried about her woes
A werewolf fate isn't one of pleasure
This girl didn't want more to share her pain
She wandered through the countryside
Looking for a place to stay
Found a nearby farm and fell asleep on the hay

She awoke hours later, expecting to find the angry owners of the farm
Yet the only face in front was that of a woman, who meant her no harm
With a pleasant smile that showed her dimples
With loose hair that wasn't shingled
She offered a hand to the lonely girl
Guided her back to her safe home

Gave her supper and some rest
The werewolf however couldn't help but fret
She had to get out, lest the moon come up
So she ran away as her wolfish side showed
Unbeknownst to her the kind woman followed
Witnessed her transformation from a girl to an abomination

Yet for the kind woman she was one soul
A soul of sadness, a soul of loneliness
She hugged the wolf with all her might
Letting her know everything will be alright

The wolf didnt howl in sadness for once
But stayed lovingly in the embrace
The new day came and as the sun shone
The lonely girl looked up to the kind girl
And realized, she may not be able to touch the moon but it mattered to her nonce

For she had found companionship in a rainbow
As the kind girl was all seven colours at once

Weeks turned into months into years
And the lonely girl ceased to exist
For she had found a kindred spirit
With whom she spent the rest of her days
Laughing and kissing, the couple was madly in love
So strong was their passion the lonely girl forgot her troubles
She kissed the kind girl fiercely and she returned the favour
And they spent the night becoming one

Yet such was the curse of the lonely girl
Come morning she looked in horror
The bite mark on the neck of her lover
This werewolf had found her prey
Marking her with love instead of hatred
But marking her all the same

Fulfilling her destiny of spreading pain the girl cried in shame
Running away from her haven
Her destiny fulfilled the moon called her back
And she permanently changed into the beast she knew she always was

For her selfish desires had caused another life to lose its joy
But not in the way she imagined

The bite mark had never bothered the kind girl for she loved the werewolf, even if she became the same
The kind girl searched for her, eventually finding the lone wolf
She cried in joy running to the wolf and kissing it's snout
Yet the wolf didnt respond the same

For the lone wolf had lost memories
As she had fulfilled her destiny and turned into this beast of pain
The kind girl wept in sorrow at the loss of her love
As night approached both of the lone wolves now howled in the pain they shared
A howl so fierce it scared away the birds
For the moon had now claimed both of them as hers.

Forever Valentine

A blush keeps creeping up on my face whenever you call me cute
It's hard to control the urge to just come swoop you up and travel together in our hidden route
Alone as we travel this vast countryside arm in arm
With the sound of your laughter in the passenger seat being my healing balm

Your face is so beautiful, a photo of which should be considered as an artistic masterpiece
Your smile so delightful, your expressions matching those of the angel that I always wanted to keep
With your round lovable eyes filled with care and mischief
With a body so gorgeous thinking about it keeps me up at night, unable to sleep
Her personality is so intriguing, her nature ever loving, perfection like that should be declared a crime
My eyes sparkle like stardust, my whole body radiates an unique kind of shine
As I think about our past, present and future with the biggest grin anyone can show

Thinking back to all the hugs we have had, the ones yet to come, the moments we still have to share, maybe even a kiss under the mistletoe

All the dances we have danced, all the melodies yet to come
All the words we have said, into our memories they are burned
Every day, hour, minute, second I spend with you makes me love you to a degree I can no longer comprehend
I just know I want you, with you all my happy moments I want to spend
You invoke emotions that are fierce but also true
Even if sometimes they may lead to me feeling blue
Just know that for every negative emotion such as jealousy or paranoia that very rarely may be induced
Your love also strives me to be a better person, filled with positive thoughts, happiness and moments that never have on such a large scale EVER been produced

I'd always better myself to be capable of being yours each year till the end of space and time, and then some more

You inspire me to work with my flaws to become a person that will always be your confidant, there just isn't any or
When it comes to who I want as my soulmate, as my second half
To have met a person like you that makes me feel like I can be capable and achieve heights of greatness, for that I am glad

So come, let's dance to this merry tune of craziness
Let's visit this abandoned town of hopes and dreams, of our regrets and laziness
Let's reignite the spark of the once lost thoughts and aspirations
Together we can do anything, screw all these rules and regulations
You feel like comfort, you feel like home, you feel like relief after surviving a never ending storm
My love for you I wanna shout to the world, my cry for you louder than any horn
So take my hand and never let go as we travel into the abyss made for you and I
We still need to write our story, the biggest romance of the generation, so don't be shy

Conundrum To Philosophy

Hand in hand we walk down this corridor
Your eyes bore into me, your head is on my shoulder
I stare lovingly at you, my love, finally requited
I spent days, I spent months, seconds, minutes felt like years
Loving you, embracing you, sometimes falling prey to my tears
Love is messy, love is selfish, love is often times hard
Yet it's all worth it, because at the end of the day you and me are no longer apart

I can't put into words the value you brought into my life
With you by my side I feel adrift in the wind, as if I'm a kite
Free from the ground, free from my troubles
Flying in the sky as the world beneath me trembles
You are a person that poses a problem to many a majority
Because you, my love, are a conundrum to philosophy
Aristotle, Socrates, Platos and Diogenes

All the old men look at you as if you are a genie
Because you are a solution to the problem they pondered on for centuries
A solution so easy, it baffles them and their ancestries

It's the little things in life that makes it so fulfilling
Your love brings so much meaning to my understanding of the universe, my emotions start spilling
With you I can be myself, nothing I need to hide
Our love story is a slow build up, the time for it I can bide
Even when we are lost we still manage to discover each other
When you came into my life, I forgot the meaning of the word 'bother'
You make my heart race, you make me melt
Our love is stronger than any weapon a blacksmith can smelt

I can still remember the day clearly, the sky seemed so blue
The day in which you told me "I like you too"
All my fears, all my insecurities, they vanished without a trace
Everything seems clearer now, I have to say I like this change of pace

Love is a two way street, I'm glad you
reciprocate
My soul feels connected, not a single trace of
any taint
Nothing can beat the beauty that is you and I
Never do I have to look at the word love and
sigh
I'm finally glad that someday our emotions can
set in motion a thing that will never end
A love story of ours, from Paris to Switzerland

Galaxy In The Universe

Sometimes I sit back and ponder
Why am I such a mess in my head
I have no clear explanation for the stress I'm under
I can't say why I sometimes feel emotionally dead

Surrounded by familiar faces, all laughing heartily in a single breath
Yet my anxiety kicks in, even amongst friends I feel as if they are plotting my death
Their faces are red from the joy they have, whole heartedly smiling
Yet I sit there with a fake smile, crying internally about my whining
I'm like a galaxy light years away, why do I feel so alone
On my worst days im more akin to a black hole, where light cannot be shone

And then you come along, creating a sparkle in this world
I hate how I love you so much as I hang on to your every word

But why would you love me ever, the way that I love you
I'm like a failed chemistry experiment, my insides are liquid ooze
I can't help but fall for you, every single day
These feelings just get stronger, when it comes to restraining them I have no say

I just wanna say, you feel like the missing piece of my puzzle
I wish to hug you every single day, cuddle next to you and nuzzle
I cant stand our distance any more, each day your warmth I miss
So far apart you're a dream away, I so badly want to steal your kiss

But what's the use of these emotions, when I'm still a cloud of dust floating in space
Maybe I should run away from everyone and everything, that notion however leaves a bad taste
As I know my heart wants you there, lying besides me underneath the sun
Being with you is a joy, I've never experienced such fun

Yet I know the love will never be the same

I sigh as I swirl in the clouds that surround me, oh what a shame
Having you is a blessing in itself, yet I can't help but be greedy
I'm an amalgam of emotions, but when it boils down to it, I guess I'm just needy

Permanently orbiting a place where it's always night
I wonder what is right
Life is an eternal Tug of war between the heart and the brain
Sometimes I'm afraid, that this war will end with me being slain

When it comes to you , there is so much secrecy
The most desired part of you, is your transparency
Yet feelings are never crystal clear, they can't be transparent
Even if I try to live in denial, some things are apparent
For people closure is necessary, to be able to move on
Yet I fear needing to have closure, never want to move on

Love is a strange feeling, even if it's unrequited it won't go away

No matter what you do, your actions still make me sway
Its difficult to explain to an outsider, how much of it is a change
When we are together, it's a whole different world, our kind of craze

You're capable of piercing a lone wolfs heart, so I don't think it's soon
To say the undisputable fact, that any wolf would love you more than the moon
Thank you for making me feel whole, atleast for a while
As I collapse into stardust once more, becoming somewhat of a messy pile
Loving you can never be a curse
Even if I'm just a tiny part of you, this galaxy still wants to be in your youniverse

Imagine

Imagine being such a person for someone that
their eyes go wide when you leave a single text
Not being able to talk to you, not being able to
be in your presence, that's a predicament which
leaves them feeling perplexed
Imagine being such a person without whom a
group feels incomplete and empty
When you are there the people become lively,
moments of happiness become aplenty

Imagine being such a person that upon hearing
your voice they get a sensation that is so
soothing
That tears start rolling down their face, comfort
they find, many types of emotions start brewing
Imagine being such a person who becomes the
only source of one's calls, the only source where
they can be open about what they are feeling
Even when they shut themselves down to the
world and act tough, talking to you makes them
finally feel like they are healing

Imagine being such a person with whom
discussing any fandom is so interesting and
fulfilling

That when you get into that craze, debate with you about it leaves a person with a smile that can only be described as booming
Imagine being such a person that even when you aren't as familiar with someone, a compliment from you can make their day
Being called pretty by you makes them feel so good about themselves, more than what any other stranger could say

Imagine being such a person with whom few talks about philosophy can leave such an impact
That when you aren't present in their life they feel inclined to call you, feel obliged to keep the short friendship still intact

Imagine being such a person who helped a lost soul discover the meaning of love
With you they can discover their true self and feel emotions that they never thought they can experience, a deep sensation that they belove
Imagine being such a person who makes another concerned with where you place them in silly things such as friendship lists
Knowing that they matter to you in these small things gives them a feeling equivalent to pure bliss

Imagine being such a person who teams up with their family to give other people sweet gifts
The smile they get from your thoughtfulness, a thoughtfulness that makes them sniff
Imagine being such a person who despises their behaviour during puberty to their parents
Even though it's normal for teenagers and many don't even regret, the amazing love you have for the people who birthed you is apparent

Imagine being such a person, so beautiful and bright
Yet a few academic issues makes you think that you are no longer a light
Imagine being such a person who despite facing problems many aspirants as well face during their career, many problems teenager as well face during their growth, feel like you are a person who's abnormal and horrible
When in fact, you being a normal kid going through issues and insecurity is more plausible

It's okay to not be okay, as an amazing person told
A person you admire, so accepting their words seem like a simple comfort for you to hold
Despite everything you should never forget the positives

Never drown yourself in an endless sea of
criticism, many of which are made up negatives

Imagine, being such a person who accepts these
things as much as they accept their flaws,
knowing at worst they are a normal human being
going through stages of life
And be determined to go through this mess with
a clear mind, not one full of negativity and
strife......

A Camp Of Our Own

I want to build with you a camp of our own
A place with you is what I will call home
When I gaze into your eyes my wishes become more clear
You are the person I love, the one I hold most dear

I wanna mess up the unbridled beauty that is your hair
I wanna take you in my arms and dance with you in the grass with our feet bare
I can sometimes never fathom that an angel like you is what I have
As I sit in the campfire besides you thinking about my past
I smile at all the silly things I did to make every moment between us last
I regret nothing I did with you for everything was so special
Every moment with you feels like an eternity, it's magical

As we go through the strawberry fields side by side

I grasp your hand firmly for I know distance
can't separate us no matter how wide
We go up to to the attic to see the oracle, the old
mummy that haunts
She tells me a prophecy I already knew, that you
are the only one I'll ever want

We go to the Big House to see the wild centaurs
From the woods come laughing Artemis's
hunters
We play together Capture The Flag
With you beside me victory is what we bag
We go to the dining pavilions and both of us
order blue coke
We gobble up so many pizzas we nearly choke
The cleaning harpies will eat us if we don't hurry
So together we go to my cabin In a flurry

Climb the roof of it and stay together, watching
the stars and the moon shine
As I wrap my arms around you knowing no
monsters can stand a chance when our strengths
together combine
I'm at peace being in your presence for you are a
healer
You may be Athena's daughter but you have
Apollo's powers when it comes to making me
feel better

Angel in Disguise

She was born without any white majestic wings
sprouting out of her back
A mission to preach in favour of a god, to be the
messenger of heaven, such a role she lacked
Neither was she a spirit nor could she fly
She felt entirely human, with normal emotions,
who could sometimes breakdown and cry

She was a girl vibrant and full of energy
With whom kind souls could find a special type
of synergy
Taking on the role of an elder sister in her life
Maybe that could explain why the desire to help
inside her was always rife

She really wasn't anything special she would tell
herself as she grew up happy and compassionate
Just a normal person with a loving family and
friends, she really was fortunate
With a smile on her face and a shining outlook
she did something so very bold
An act that humans usually do, the silly act of
growing old

Responsibility became her forte as school took a center stage
The kind soul helped in every way she could, even becoming a class representative
With her beautiful mind and pondering thoughts she explored the possibilities of future, seeking out dreams and a goal
Following in her family's footsteps to be a doctor and help people, now that is something that appealed to her kind soul

In this vortex of life things are ever changing
One moment leads to the next forming a picture not quite envisioned, something the creator finds entertaining
A doctor's path isn't easy as the kind soul trudged through an academic hell
The vortex of her life began distorting as well when they rang the eleventh grade bell

The figure of adults took on an unfamiliar shape as the infallible beings suddenly made evident their flaws
The whole life seems to become a wild west in the absence of your mind's established universal laws
Things get confusing, self identity is convulsing
Some friendships turn out to be so toxic they can become very suffocating

The kind girl went through it all, as did her peers
It is quite disheartening when no longer are
fairytale monsters topping the list of your fears

So many changes yet not one concrete reason
For academic hell is but just one aspect in this
weird season
Somewhere between this time the girl started to
feel more and more lost in her prison of a mind
The feeling of being beautiful started to elude
her as towards her enthralling beauty she
became blind
Looking into the mirror she was oblivious to the
golden halo on top of her head as she looked on
with a scorn
For in her eyes all she could see were bright red
devil's horns

Time passes by slowly now, taking the form of
sand in an hourglass
With trials and tribulations comes knowledge of
which bonds are worth it, which ones are meant
to last
Growing from experiences yet still conflicted in
her mind she has her group of close friends
People that to her are worth it as she lunges
forward to hold their hands
One particular set of hands she finds quite
peculiar

Embarking on a journey with that person she
experiences feelings that are quite unfamiliar
Feelings that take time for her to figure out what
they entail
As the realisation that she can actually
experience the emotion of falling in love
prevails

Truly who she is right now is someone she
herself finds unpredictable
Never in a million years did she imagine herself
to be in the situation into which she has now
stumbled
She's nothing special is a proclamation in which
she chooses to still revel
Yet now she is met with resistance from another
person for whom she defines the word special on
a whole other scale and level

Circumstances change and the whole world is
thrown into chaos and disarray
Yet underneath all this for many people she
continues to be a source of warmth, with that
one particular person especially enjoying the
sunlight of her benevolent ray
With a sigh the girl looks at all of her
surroundings
At a life that keeps on rebounding
For she has a family that's still there

Friends that still care
A person who's heart she got to possess
Over all of her flaws and virtues that fool chooses to obsess

She's a person who continuously is a source of help for others
Maybe her negativities aren't really a thing of bother, she begins to ponder
For she's now nineteen, the number that signifies knowledge, spirituality, success, wisdom, breakthrough and new beginnings
So even though growing old can be a woe new sprouts in her garden right now are still springing
So with happiness the ones who love her wait as time they bide
For the moment where the kind girl will eventually realise through her bonds and self enlightenment, that despite everything, she is an angel in disguise.....

Leap of Faith

When the world feels like it wants to punish you
I'd grab your hand
Doing what needs to be done feels akin to finding an oasis in the desert, some water and trees among the sand
It's difficult for you to even fathom coming into this situation
Much less actually succeeding and finding your salvation

But faith can move mountains it is said
Yet the fear of falling would still fill one with dread
The trepidation is immense and the body feels paralysed
Jumping the long distance isn't something you're really cut out for you think to yourself as you are terrorized

Honestly all I can offer you is my reassurance and love
Which I know isn't enough proof to make you think you can actually fly like a dove
So here I am on my knees requesting the impossible

To ignore the warnings of your conscience, have faith and finally become unstoppable

The gap feels too big to take a jump
The cliff is too steep and looking below you just become too scared of the plunge
But never alone you will be during this journey of the century
A pack of two we will be famous across the country

Truly I can't really hypothesise someone else I'd like to be with
You've spoiled me so much that heaven no longer seems a myth
Who else could hug so eloquently the way you do
Your back hugs take me to cloud nine that much is true
The scenery I see in your eyes makes the rest of the world feel grey and dull
The sound of your voice being so soothing it can be compared to a siren's lull

I know you feel as if you're in denial of the fact that life is ultimately meaningless and irrelevant
But when experiencing such moments, how else can you describe them other than elegant?

If these small ripples in the ocean can make us so happy and fulfilled
Then the waves crashing down upon us can hardly destroy something this beautiful

At the end of the day all these words just sound like a pleasant melody
Easy enough to forget after removing your earphones and drowning yourself in melancholy
You fear as if your inner self is too destructive and violent to ever let peace last
In one moment all of this can be taken away with a single blast
So fearful you are of letting yourself stay in my embrace
Wondering whether I'll be better off if you disappear without a trace

But even if you don't currently I do indeed have faith
That things would slowly come together, no need for such haste
For I know for sure one day you will indeed take the chance
Of crossing to the other side to join me in a dance
As we get trapped in a trance

From these moments of darkness and doubt you shall advance

It isn't easy to not be uneasy with love when you feel you shouldn't be loved
But despite our dashing looks we actually aren't that flammable that we will turn into dust
So I'll be always cheering you on as you continue to make me proud and prouder
The voice of your soul I shall always endeavour to hear as it only will become loud and louder
For I shall always be by your side, extending my hand and waiting for your leap
Because one leap of faith is all it would take to make you realise I am indeed yours to keep

And even if you should fail and falter at making the jump to the other side
I'll come right back to your side and time I shall bide
For you to realise you're indeed worthy of being beautiful and having beauty
You, the one with the mesmerising face and hair that smells fruity
Have all the time you need and breaks you require
To get the confidence that is by right yours to acquire
For I want to hold your hand always and forever

As I do love you fervently it's enough to make me always want to stay together
So a solemn promise I make to you while you're still willing to be awake
That to conquer this height a single leap of faith towards me is all it would take....

Love Inspired

Seeking inspiration is a common human act
And inspiration comes in forms a plenty
Often we are inspired by those who show it's
possible to keep our inner strength intact
And those are the kinds of people who are able
to love others absolutely

Love often blossoms in its purest form in the
number of two
Spending years with your soulmate as the
concept of being in a paradise was brewed
So evident their passion is that their unity was
forever maintained
Look past their little fights, their teasings, and
you will discover an extreme level of
understanding and affection that remained

Maybe being their child makes me biased
towards the way I perceive their bond
But it doesn't change the fact that my parents
together are as strong as iron and bronze
Truly fascinating it is as my young soul fathoms
how love can last so many years after it's birth
When usually love can be observed to fade away
pretty quickly in so many places of our Earth

The concept of generation gap arises between
the parents and children
Therefore the concept of love also undergoes
many other definitions
Teased are the old ones for their outdated views
as the younglings put forward their idealism
But lost in this whole debate is the fact, that
indifferent to all the arguments being put
forward, my parent's love is still something that
maintains the concept of realism

From drinking the morning tea together to
scolding me and my brother at dinner
From going on trips together to holding each
other's hands and feeling like winners
From looking after their children together to
watching them advance in their life
From meeting each other for the first time to
becoming husband and wife

Being in love is more akin to strength rather than
being a weakness as some cynics claim
And to prove the former to me, seems something
that my parents had as one of their aims
25 years of togetherness and love seems
impossible to me, it must be a myth the concept
of a 'Silver Jubilee'

Yet, here are my parents, once again celebrating
with love and affection, their anniversary

So to harken back to the beginning, it is with
utmost sincerity and adoration
That I find my parents and their love, a big
source of inspiration
For being one for so long is an achievement and
is strength that deserves to be applauded
So therefore I'd always like to have this love and
it's importance in my life, celebrated❤

An Ode To Your Wedding

A brother-sister bond is something that is considered incredibly special
So having to deal with four brothers in the same house must have been quite exponential
Between all the small fights and silly behaviour by us four brothers
You've always been patient and sweet with us, you've always been quite an exceptional mediator
And as we grew up and became a bit more mature
You were still there for us in moments when regarding life we were still unsure

Too many sweet memories with you which I'll always remember fondly
Spending time with you always proves to be so much fun because you are always jolly
One thing in particular that I especially have carved into my mind
Is enjoying a popcorn Bollywood movie with you, the one's I'd usually hate but in your presence they became less of a grind

Playing Badminton with you gave me a new appreciation for the sport even though you were the one who managed to get the last score
But sis let me remind you, when it comes to Ludo our score is still Nine to Four
You'd never be able to defeat my reverse psychology in that game so better to accept the defeat
But still if you want to play another game of Ludo I'm down to have my victory repeat

So, being at your big day I couldn't be more happier for you as you deserve all the love and affection
As I look back towards all the teasing I used to do regarding this to your frustration
Annoying you with all the names of the guys in your college but in the end you had the last laugh
As the person you found is so much better on every graph!
When it finally comes down to it, your wedding is a day that will go down in history books with pride
As it will be the day featuring the most beautiful bride

From having a back and forth with me in every
silly love conversation we had and making
everyone in our house laugh so much
To being at your wedding as your love journey
begins and having my heart touched
I'd like to conclude this poem by saying
something you already know but needs to be
said more
Your brothers will always be there for you
whenever you feel sore❤

My Insurgents

To be honest not really sure how to start a poem
about yours truly
Really confused on how to write something that
will fulfill my best friend duty
Probably just going to splatter my thoughts onto
this, as is how things roll
For one thing is certain, without you guys my
school life wouldn't have felt whole

To start with the annoying one I swear you were
infuriating with your behaviour and good looks
Driving all of us crazy as every guy tried to get
through us to be in your good books
But you were a person that despite all the
spotlight
Became a sweetheart and akin to a bulb that was
way too bright
One thing that is underrated about you is your
smile
It's really a smile that makes you want to remain
friends, to always go the extra mile
Sometimes during the marathon we may get left
behind

But despite on and offs, friendship might not seeming the same, we come back to the same pace, kudos to our mind

But really talking about you can never be complete without talking about the love of your life
Not talking about your partners, but about your dog that I'd be willing to protect with a knife
You enjoy making us jealous with that shitzu don't you as you look down upon us dogless lonely souls with the biggest grin
But honestly who can ever fault you, with a dog that pretty you have conquered life and turned it into a huge win

To talk about the irritating one, you definitely are a best friend that I can confide in and get great advice and lots of love and support
Even if many of your antics and lame jokes makes me wanna snort
To speak nothing of how strong your mental state is with all the adversaries you face
You still remain the most compassionate, no doubt being a person many girls will chase
You have my love and support always and I know I always have your loyalty

As I sit back and see you advance in your career,
no doubt in the future you shall be seen as
royalty

To talk about the infuriating one, geez are you
always ready to wrestle
Having the most direct approach to life as when
you walk the land itself seems to rumble
But beneath the tough but fun exterior of the
tomboy
You have a sweet Bollywood romantic heart that
yearns for compassion and joy
You have a temper that's fatal but a heart that's
loyal
Being such a vibrant being to our group which
can be compared to a plant while you are the soil

To talk about the exasperating one, honestly you
can't be described as anything less than stellar
Without a doubt being such an important piece
to the puzzle as for our group you are the pillar
You have an artistic mind, something that I
adore as you write words that are meaningful
and paint art that is beautiful
Maybe that is why you have been able to always
provide love that is so bountiful...

I look at our group of five

I look at all of our love for each other continuing to thrive
When it boils down to it, truly I am just grateful
To have such an amazing group of friends who for all their faults, are absolutely beautiful
Being the person I am I don't think I'm an easy person to like
But you guys seem determined to love me even after my three strikes
So I'll just let go of all my complaints for now and join your embrace
As I cherish the bond we have and the trials we endured to survive with such elegance and grace
From my deepest corners of soul, peace and happiness be emergent
When I think of all five of us together, a pack of insurgents ❤

Bittersweet Farewell

Sometimes it's difficult to accept the inevitable
until it's right up your face
Living in denial seems the most humane thing to
do in this case
Winnie the Pooh said you are my favourite hello
and hardest goodbye
He may be a childhood character but that line
hits hard enough in a situation like this to make
one cry

Farewells can be painful for you have to bid
adieu to a loved one
Or they can be happy as you are finally
separated from pain, all the toxicity is final and
done
In this case it feels bittersweet, for it is an
amalgam of the above
Too bitter to let a loved one go but happy for the
chance of a new phase to start hereof

Truth to be told there's so much that still feels it
needs to be done and addressed
Hey I can't even cook properly as of now, I need
time to learn it at your behest

There's so much I need to learn so I can grow up and become mature
So of course I can't bid you farewell because the upcoming challenges together I want to endure

I need you to strengthen your faith in me so a farewell shouldn't be on the cards
Saying goodbye right now feels like too massive of a bombard
Miles away would you still trust in me enough to not let this bond harden?
For quite literally as of now I can't even plant flowers in the garden
How can you even hope for me to cultivate something as beautiful as this
But the trick is slowly watering them, isn't it?
A drop one day and another the next
Hang in we will, even if we need to rely on text

With a heavy heart I look to the future which I know will be tough and unyielding
A game of patience, perseverance and strength shall be proceeding
For someday soon we shall have our hearts desire
Succeed we shall as we move forward in life and climb even higher

I'm not really ready but I take a deep breath and sigh
Doesn't matter I feel as the time is finally nigh
For us to look past the past and all the sins
As a new phase of our lives, will finally begin

www.ingramcontent.com/pod-product-compliance
Lightning Source LLC
Chambersburg PA
CBHW051734130826
49812CB00033B/852
* 9 7 8 9 3 5 7 2 1 0 7 0 6 *